Robert Weir

Uncle Samuels Whistle and What it Costs

Robert Weir

Uncle Samuels Whistle and What it Costs

ISBN/EAN: 9783743373105

Manufactured in Europe, USA, Canada, Australia, Japa

Cover: Foto ©ninafisch / pixelio.de

Manufactured and distributed by brebook publishing software
(www.brebook.com)

Robert Weir

Uncle Samuels Whistle and What it Costs

UNCLE SAMUEL'S WHISTLE;

And what it Costs.

A TALE.

"He whistled as he went, for want of thought."—DRYDEN.

"So long as a man rides his hobby-horse peaceably and quietly along the king's highway, and neither compels you nor me to get up behind him, pray, sir, what have either you or I to do with it?"—TRISTAM SHANDY, chap. vii.

—

"But what shall we do, when he not only forces us to get up behind him, but makes us pay for the ride?"—CITIZEN'S CURRENT INQUIRY.

Hatching the Egg.

I.

It was a lovely summer morning, in the old days of peace. A cloudless blue sky bent over the glittering metropolis—a bright sun flooded its busy streets with splendor—and a gentle wind made music in the trees that grace its parks and causeways. The haunts, alike of labor and of pleasure, were already thronged. Up and down Broadway and the Avenues, surged the customary tide of human beings. Horse-cars rumbled and jingled along their various tracks, and stages, carriages, carts, and drays added volume and variety to the din of city life. All was light—activity—animation.

Especially in the City Hall Park!

There were no soldiers then in that verdurous region; nor barracks, nor recruiting tents, nor hospitals, nor artillery, nor vestiges of the "circumstance of glorious war." But the peaceful grass grew there untrampled, and birds flitted from tree to tree; and the fountain, which Mr. N. P. Willis has commemorated in song, played away in the cool and sparkling fashion peculiar to fountains; and the baked Jersey mud statue of General Washington—erected by a considerate posterity for the accommodation of the sculptor—gazed placidly at the City Hall, or seemed to smile upon the comfortable enterprise of those youthful Bohemians who thrive by polishing the boots of respectability. A scene of pastoral innocence and beauty!

Amidst that scene, and near the base of that imposing monument, there stood, on the lovely morning previously referred to, a man. He was wrapped in profound thought—and in seedy garments. His face was pale, and wore the expression of intellect tempered by timidity. His black clothes, though they had been carefully brushed, presented that glazed appearance which, except, perhaps, in the case of satinet, is the unmistakable evidence of age. His hat was greasy—his boots were soiled with dust. In his right hand he grasped a heavy walking stick: in his left, a huge roll of white paper. And so he stood—now glancing at the City Hall clock, now at the stately edifice, towards the south-east, whence issue, daily and weekly, so many organs of public opinion, in the shape of newspapers.

He had waited there already during nearly two hours—a spectacle of superfluous patience, exciting the suspicion of neighboring police officers, and stirring up the ire of contiguous apple-women. For he seemed to have no legitimate calling, and he certainly bought no apples. Nor did he incline the ear of attention to the tattered youths who repeatedly said to him, "blag yer boots." The seedy man was plainly pre-occupied, and intent on serious things.

At length, as the bell tolled the hour of ten, the stranger emerged from his reverie, walked rapidly from the Washington statue, and disappeared within the principal edifice of Printing House Square.— Let us follow his footsteps.

We shall find him in a spacious and handsome office, adorned with a large library, and with pictures, chiefly of a marine character. A close examination of the library would disclose many books of a scientific kind, such as "Mariotte's Law" and "Isherwood's Engineering Precedents;" and mingled with these, divers volumes of poetry and

Belles Lettres, showing that their owner, however devoted to science, is yet addicted to occasional indulgence in "Shakspeare and the musical glasses." The other appointments of this room are correspondingly sumptuous. The carpet is rich and soft—the furniture is carved and valuable. In the centre of the apartment stands a handsome writing-table, littered with papers and drawings. Near this, in a comfortable arm chair, sits a man of singular appearance, and, as the reader will presently perceive, of still more singular talents. He is the hero of this tale.

The Hero of Dash-pots and the seedy Inventor.

To him has entered the seedy stranger. . . . They talk.

"I am an inventor, sir,—a poor man; but I have a fortune in these plans. You are rich—you are influential. I have come to ask your aid in presenting my invention to the notice of the United States Navy Department."

"What is your name, sir? and what is the nature of your invention?"

B

"My name, sir, is *Sickles*——. My invention is a steam cut-off for application to marine engines."

"Sir," said the great man, "you have come to the right shop. My foot is on my native heath, and my name is D*ickinso*n."

The seedy inventor bowed, and deposited his roll of paper upon the table. *ickinson*

"Sit, my friend," said the magnanimous D———n. "I will cast my eye over your drawings. The subject of economizing steam and coal has long been familiar to my thoughts. I am a devout student of Watt, and I know all about water. Mariotte is my *vade mecum*, and I abhor the very name of Isherwood. (A.) Likewise, I am a reader of the Hebrew melodies of the gifted Lord Byron. I will read them to you, if you like; but not immediately. Amuse yourself for a few moments, while I glance at these papers."

The inventor again bowed, sat down, and picking up a pamphlet, devoted his mind to the *"Tenth Annual Report of the Board of Water Commissioners to the Common Council of the City of Detroit."* (B.)

Let us not dwell upon what he found therein; at least not yet. Suffice it to say, that he had not long to read nor long to wait for the reply of his heroic companion.

"I will take this invention, sir, under my patronage and supervision. It is not exhaustive, but it is a step in advance. So far as it goes, it harmonizes with my own views. But I warn you beforehand, that mighty obstacles must be overcome ere it can be made a practical success. Be re-assured, however! Those obstacles are not invulnerable. It was, as remarked by the erudite Game Chicken, "within the resources of science to double up Mr. Dombey:" it is equally within the resources of science to double up Isherwood. (C.) That fellow is very destructive on coals, and it is high time that something were done about it. I behold in this cut-off the immediate means of doing something. I will let loose upon the Navy Department the entire strength of my inspiration—the whole vast power of Mariotte's Law and of Lord Byron's melodies. Nay, sir, I will even press Shakspeare into this service. So shall the cut-off carry the day. Trust yours truly for that. But, in the meanwhile, we must agree, sir, upon terms—upon terms, sir, and conditions. A cut-off is, as it were, a machine; but, as noticed by the subtle Mr. Hazlitt, a man of genius is not.—Modesty forbids me to employ more definite language. I see in your intelligent countenance that you perceive the application of this remark. I shall stipulate, sir, for an interest in this invention—an interest of liberal scope and of large possible value. Upon that wall, before you, hangs a map of the United States of America, a great and glorious Republic, my friend, founded at an early period by the Father of his Country, and popularly known as an asylum for the oppressed of all nations. Those States, sir, are numerous and wealthy. Those upon the northern Atlantic sea-board are peculiarly so. I stipulate for the exclusive right of applying this invention in those States. I appropriate to myself New England, New York, Pennsylvania, the Middle States, and those that extend westward along the lakes. The remainder I leave to you. Accept these terms, and I lift you at once from the slough of obscurity to the heights of fame. Reject them, and I leave you to chance.

> 'There is a tide in the affairs of men,
> Which, taken at the flood, leads on to fortune.'

That tide, sir, is now at the flood with you. Will you take it or no? I pause for a reply."

The seedy inventor, overwhelmed by this eloquence, could only bow and point to his plans.

"I accept the terms, sir," he said, at length, "and leave my fate in your hands."

"In my hands," responded the heroic D———n, "your fate is glory. You have heard, no doubt, of the star of purest ray serene. I am that star. Henceforth it will be my vocation to shine upon you. Be happy in that reflection! And now, sir, before we part, permit me to read a paraphrase of one of those Byronic melodies to which I have made allusion. Its application will, I think, be sufficiently evident. Here it is: (D.)

> I walk in lonely beauty bright!
>   The breath of steam around me flies;
> And, radiant in metallic light,
>   I see the brazen dash-pots rise—
> A vision, glorious to my sight
>   As purple peaks of Paradise!
>
> One pot the more, one pot the less,
>   Would make no difference in the view;
> For all that's best of loveliness,
>   And all that's best of science too,
> Are garnered up, mankind to bless,
>   In dash-pots of the brazen hue.
>
> The happy thought around me coils,
>   And cheers me on at every turn;
> While engine-drivers pour their oils,
>   And stokers make their coals to burn;
> That I appropriate the spoils
>   Within my dash-pot's portly urn!

"There, my friend," added this bard of science and of dash-pots, "that will suffice. You are now acquainted with me, and with my sentiments. *Haec olim meminisse juvabit.* Leave me your address. I shall write to you from Washington City—from the capital—whither my steps now tend. Consider the cut-off a fixed fact. I will not say that I shall not improve upon your design. *Non tetigit, non ornavit.* But its success is all the more certain. Give me your hand, sir. Good morning!"

The dilapidated inventor withdrew, and the hero was left alone. A moment he seemed transfixed as by a mighty thought; then his tall form relaxed, and he sank back into the arm chair and closed his eyes. The recent effort of eloquence had overpowered him. The great man slept—slept and dreamed.

And this was his vision.

D——n's Dream of Triumph.

A golden cloud seemed floating in mid-air, upborne at its four corners by Watt and Mariotte, Brunel and Samuel Smiles. Upon that cloud rested an enormous throne, made of variously colored and strongly welded dash-pots. Upon that throne, in royal state, sat the august D———n. At his feet, and serving for a footstool, appeared the scientific writings of the hated Isherwood. In his hands was upreared a gigantic brazen dash-pot, whereinto fell a continual shower of golden eagles, poured from above by Clio, the muse of history,—a figure, however, closely resembling that of Secretary *Touely* Around him, in every direction, floated the shapes of war-vessels, provided with the S*ickle*s cut-off. Beneath the cloud, on which rested this imposing monarchy, appeared the wretchéd Isherwood and the Water Commissioners of Detroit, pendant, heads downward, and grasping frantically at nothing. A gentle breeze, as of windy and ever-blowing Fame, impélled this pageant through the heavens. And thus the sleeper beheld, prefigured in light and shadow, his own immortality.

II.

Washington, D. C., —— —, 18—.

My Dear S——s:

Veni! vidi! vici! So said the great Roman, after victory. So says the engineer of the period, under similar circumstances.

It was, nevertheless, an achievement of magnitude and of difficulty. Prejudice, of deep root and of long continuance, opposed me at the outset. Conventionality, embodied in the form of a naval official, frowned darkly upon the champion of progress, your humble friend. Old ideas of economy—the crude notions of our antiquated forefathers —arose before me, like battle lines in Parisian streets, before the footsteps of Revolution. But, like Revolution, I nevertheless swept onward, bearing down prejudice, conventionality, and old ideas. Accordingly, these latter are dust, and I am jubilant.

Never shall I forget that memorable morning, when, with miniature dash-pot in one hand, and gilt-edged copy of "Mariotte's Law" in the other, I made my final effectual appeal to the Secretary of the Navy. Like an oracle I stood before him; and it is no exaggeration to say that I forced conviction upon his mind, with an energy and a righteous violence that literally withered him in his official arm chair. At first, I dwelt upon the simple principle of the cut-off. Then, incidentally, I gave him a detailed account of the life and services of James Watt. From this theme, by an easy and natural transition, I advanced to speak of myself; and, as is not usual with mankind, I made the most of the subject. I described, with scientific prolixity and minuteness, my own novel machinery, my improvements upon the clever, though crude, idea of your active, ambitious and promising mind; and into this description I introduced, with much effect, my celebrated paraphrase of a Hebrew melody, celebrating the dash-pot. Lastly, in a peroration, worthy, though I say it, of the Ciceronian age, I called upon him to submit to the eternal laws of the Universe, as illustrated in my authentic teachings. "Respect the divine law," I exclaimed, "of which I am but the humble representative! You may think to escape its power for a time, but you must surely submit to it at last. Yield, therefore, without fruitless resistance. Do what you will, you cannot get far ahead of the old man up above. Even Isherwood, with all his gold lace and all his money, can avail you nothing. The laws of expansion operate without regard to Isherwood. I have placed his book on a cylinder-head of one of my engines, and it never made the least difference in the operation of the piston. Will you, then, be stayed on the noble road of progress by the voice of a quack and a beast, a knave and a wretch—

> A villain,
> A cut-purse of the empire and the rule,
> Who from the shelf the precious diadem stole,
> And put it in his pocket?

Will you butt your head against a stone wall, because, like the man in the novel, you find it "so very satisfying"? No, you will not! Or, if a stone wall is to be butted, you will rather choose that it be the penetrable stone wall of man's ignorance, than the indomitable barrier of eternal law. You will be mindful of the sage fortitude of the pious American citizen of African descent, who said that when de Lord told him to butt a hole through a stone wall, it was his business to butt, and de Lord's business to carry him through. You will think of this, I say; and if Isherwood be powerful, you will be consoled by the reflection that all human power is weak against the power of Nature. And so, side by side with me, you will keep on butting."

"D———n," said the Secretary, when I thus concluded my harangue, "you are a great man. Take a chair, and let 's liquor. I shall believe in dash pots as long as I live; and you shall build us a new war ship."

" But Isherwood is my foe."

"Isherwood be ———."

We drank some straw-colored liquor, with our mouths, after that, and so our interview terminated.

And now the PENSACOLA is in progress of construction. The egg upon which long ago we commenced to brood, will soon break, and enable us to count our chickens—chickens of iron they will be to others, my friend—Mother Cary's chickens—but to us, chickens of gold!

> "Swift fly the years, and rise th' expected morn!"

We began our work on this ship in 1858. It is now 1863. She will soon be finished, with the cut-off, and the novel machinery all complete, and I shall expect her to make such time as never was made before, by any craft of equal size and pretension. To-day, by way of verifying Mariotte's Law, I have applied the cut-off principle to her stern, and have had the stern cut-off. The effect was rending, and I witnessed it with emotions of awe. To-morrow we shall put the stern on again. Having satisfied the Law, we must now disappoint and effectually dispose of the prophets—these latter, collected here in great numbers by the malignant Isherwood, having stated that our ship will be good for nothing without a stern. As if the erudite D————n didn't recognise stern necessity.

The Department recognises it, at any rate— for I have sent in my bill. All the clerks have been, for several weeks, busy in investigating the accounts: and poor creatures!—they are quite at their wits' ends. It is a comfort to think that they did'nt have far to go. As a final resort, they have procured a calculating machine. But calculating machines are vain as against dash-pots. The ship will cost $800,000 at the very least, and the Department will have to pay it.

Isherwood, I hear, suggests that such a ship ought not to cost more than $120,000, or, at furthest, more than $140,000. Strange that people will so cling to the delusions of the past. Because old-fashioned ships and engines have been built for little or nothing, is it imagined that the scientific marvels of the future are to be got without money and without price? Perish the mercenary idea—ignoble prejudice of most ignoble minds!

Indignation devours me quite.

I can no more,

D————N.

P. S.

Several Days Later.—The great work is finished. The Ship has been tried, and a competent committee reports to the Navy Department that she is considered safe to run down the Potomac with the tide. *Go Triumphe!*   D.

c

III.

Rumor—*ac spem fronte serenat*—had often borne to my ears the musical name of D———n, the engineer. His engines, with the celebrated ——— cut-off, had been described to me—by a pious clerk in the Navy Department—as "Chief among ten thousand, and altogether lovely." As a natural consequence, I had longed to behold a specimen of the great man's art. And now the golden opportunity had come. I was at Washington. So was the Pensacola, on board which an old friend of mine held the office of Chief Engineer. She was furnished with a D———n engine. She would sail at nightfall. I did not hesitate. As the sun descended into the west, I descended into the grimy but gold-laced presence of my friend the Engineer.

First glimpse of the Engine-room.

On entering the engine-room, I was filled with amazement, not wholly unmingled with consternation. On every side, as far as the eye could reach, I beheld metallic evidences of the ingenuity of D———n. With a slight effort of fancy, I might have believed myself in a museum of mechanical curiosities. The cloud of witnesses, spoken of in Holy Writ, would be as mere vapor to the dense cloud of wheels which I then beheld. In fact, the very air was black with cogs.

> Cogs to the right of me,
> Cogs to the left of me,
> Handles and monkey-tails,
> Bristled and bothered.

One wheel, in particular, presently fixed my attention. "That," said my companion, " is the reversing wheel. It adjusts the link, for going ahead, stopping, or backing. Those only can work it, however, who understand how to manipulate the cut-off implements. You will see presently. It isn't every body that's up to science, in these days."

At this moment the Captain's bell signalled to start the engine. Simultaneously twelve men joined us on the platform. The area of this latter being about two square yards, we were conscious of being crowded.

" These hands will help us," said the Engineer.

" It appears," said I, " that science still has a few representatives extant."

" A select few," he answered ; " they have received instructions from D———n himself. Now, boys, start her."

The boys distributed themselves among the cogs, and resolutely commenced operations. I silently admired their resolution.

" Take it easy, boys," said a Lieutenant, looking in at this juncture. " The Captain's gone ashore, to buy a photograph of D———n ; he'll be on board again in half-an-hour. If you begin now, you'll get started by the time he gets back."

They began.

Two men stationed themselves at the water-valves; two went to the injection-valves ; six assumed charge of the link ; one fixed his eyes on the thermometer ; one, in a corner, drank something out of a black bottle. The Engineer himself wound up the clock. I helped him. Six more men then came in, variously armed with handspikes, beetles, hydraulic jacks, oil cans, and wrenches. A number of small boys, all in uniform, also made their appearance, bearing buckets of water, more oil cans, and several crow-bars. They stationed themselves at the dash-pots.

"I think she will start," said I to the Engineer. " Probably," said the Engineer to me.

Starting the Engine—and the Engineers.

So saying, he pushed with tremendous strength upon a monkey-tail. This latter, I noticed, was connected by rods and bell-crank levers with the valve spindle. Being pushed, it had, in course of time, the effect of opening a passover-valve—an auxiliary arrangement for working the engine by hand.

Tripping-Valves.

"The thermometer marks 153° in the shade," said a vigilant assistant.

"All right," said the Engineer. "Lend me that black bottle," he added, addressing the man in the corner. Receiving the bottle, he drank from it for five minutes.

By this time the small boys had poured several gallons of oil into the dash-pots, and had gone out for more. The men with bars and beetles had also made a vigorous attack on the valves. Several wheels were observed to be in motion. So was the man in the corner. He reeled from side to side, as if with excessive delight at the busy scene before him. Then he suddenly fell backwards down a neighboring hatch-way.

"He has forgotten his bottle," said the Engineer.

A terrific crash was now heard. The link was down—the water valves were in operation—the engine had started.

"I think they'll cast off the lines in ten minutes," remarked a small boy near me, at the same time oversetting a bucket of water. "We shant move much at first," he added. "'Taint science to move."

I now understood the crash. The piston-rod of one cylinder had reached its dead centre, making an awful noise. The men at the water-valves redoubled their exertions. The piston-rod of the other cylinder met its centre with a yet louder bang. Boys returned, with oil for the dash pots. The Engineer tugged at his monkey-tail. The injection-valves were knocked open with handspikes. The Lieutenant re-appeared, and announced the return of the Captain.

"He's got a capital picture of D———n," said this officer. "It's along with a sketch of the wings of Icarus."

"I'll go and see it," remarked the Engineer. "We shall have to wait some time, for a vacuum. Boys, put lots of oil in those dash-pots."

He went away, leaving the black bottle. I took charge of it. Also I wound up the clock, which, by this time, had run down. The man with the thermometer announced that instrument as marking 154°.

"It's warm," he said.

In ten minutes the Engineer came back. There was, as he had predicted, a vacuum, and we were in motion. The men seemed weary, but they were certainly determined. I encouraged them by circulating the black bottle.

Thus we started, and thus we were propelled. During the entire watch, the workers in the engine-room never flagged. Regularly, as did the angels upon Jacob's ladder, the boys, with their oil cans, ascended and descended. Regularly the link-men tugged at their wheel. Regularly the hammers rose and fell. Never were heroic exertions attended with more amazing results. On every side cogs grated and monkey-tail frisked in air. Crash! went the engine: bang! bang! zip!

zip! crash! bang! bang! zip! zip! And faintly through the din, I heard the voices of dash-pot men, crying for monkey-wrenches.

"Hurrah!" roared a small boy, from a neighboring dash-pot: "it's as good as fire-works on the Fourth of July—aint it, Mister?"

I did not hesitate to endorse the opinion of the small boy.

At this moment, the Captain rang "two bells." There was an immediate sensation in the engine-room.

"Cut off steam to the ninety-nine hundredth part of the stroke," roared the Engineer. "Stand by there, with sledge-hammers over the dash-pots! Put steam on the reversing-cylinder!"

But the link would not budge; and, in spite of closed throttle, the mill went tearing on. It is not easy to stay the march of science!

"Heave away on that wheel!" cried the Engineer. "Send all the firemen here, and call the other divisions! Heave with those crow-bars, and trip the valves!"

This time success. The link arose, with unearthly shrieks and groans; and the engine was stopped, as if never to move again.

Going on Watch.   Coming off.

The black bottle being empty, we all drew a long breath—and wished it were full.

"Come away," said the Engineer. "Jenkins will start her; I'm tired."

The bell rang as we left the engine-room. The terrible noise recommenced, and science, under the guidance of Jenkins, once more impelled us forward at a conservative rate.

"O that D———n were here to see!" I exclaimed, taking the Engineer's arm.

"O that he were here to feel!" was his rejoinder, the thermometer being at 154°.

I looked steadfastly upon my companion. He did not appear to advantage. It would not be too much to say that science had used him up. Moreover, he was manifestly disgusted with circumstances.

"D———n is a great man," he said. "Wait till I fill this bottle, and we'll talk it over."

A Little Oil Necessary.

I waited. We nourished ourselves. Then we sat down on a gun-carriage: and this is what the Engineer said:

"D———n is a great man. I've read his Washington speech, all about the Navy, and I know by that his mighty intellect. He's acquainted with Lord Byron's verses, and with Pope and Shakspeare; and he knows all about Mariotte's Law. This is one of his engines—with the ——— cut-off. It makes 35 revolutions a minute, and it also makes a splendid noise. These are the least of its merits. It is an admirable consumer of oil. I suppose D———n learned the value of lubrication when he was a lawyer and used to oil the bench. The usual allowance to this engine is five gallons an hour—which is'nt enough, and so the boys smuggle it on, at the rate of about a hundred and twenty-five gallons a-day. All the journals require it constantly (no pun intended). And then the firemen! It keeps them as busy as bees, because, you know, if the cut-off should become deranged—as I do sometimes, for instance—and steam should be used at full stroke on the engines, then the expansion application, through good fires, would rest entirely upon them. That is clear, is'nt it? When the engine is used at full stroke, and there are fifteen pounds of steam in the boilers, five revolutions will reduce the pressure to nine pounds. This again shows the wonderful utility of the cut-off, which saves the expense of large boilers for marine engines. D———n, as I said before, is a great man—a gigantic and tremendous man. I have read his tribute to Watt (E), and Watt, if he wots any thing about it, ought to be very grateful for such a first-class notice; and I have read also his re-

He Smuggled the Oil.

marks on expansion. And, trusting in D———n, I don't see why a donkey-boiler would'nt do for this ship, just as well as the two big ones that we carry now. But that's a point for science to determine, after we've got rid of the superfluous coal."

At this point the Engineer's remarks were interrupted by a sudden commotion in the engine-room, wherefrom, presently, several men emerged, bearing the insensible body of an oiler who had just fainted among the dash-pots. They carried him away.

"It occurs frequently," resumed my companion. "Even D———n himself became a victim once—in Jerome's yacht, I think. Science

D

must have its martyrs, you know. I 've lost several fingers myself, tripping valves; and I know three engineers who, while on duty, have dropped insensible at their posts. You will notice that our stokers are very like skeletons. Thin men stand the heat better than fat ones; and the thermometer in our engine-room rarely marks less than 140°. This is another of the beauties of the cut-off—it paves the way to promotion in the service, by cutting off so many human obstacles."

The Oiler comes on Watch.   He Watches.

Here my companion (or was I deceived in the dim moonlight?) deliberately winked upon me with one eye. Then, seizing the black bottle, he drank, with his mouth, for some time. Finally he resumed his remarks :

"D———n is a modest man, too. All great genius exhibits that characteristic. He never blows his own horn. He said once, that he 'was profoundly ignorant of a steam-engine, and supposed a cylinder-head to be a full moon.' That was modesty! No one, who has ever heard our cylinders work, would credit it of him. They suggest any thing but moons. Meteors, accompanied by thunder, would much better typify them. But whatever may be the great man's notion as to cylinder-heads, he has certainly got very clear ideas on the subject of DASH-POTS. Look at that engine, for instance! It 's all over dash-pots. They gleam like the brass kettle of by-gone days, in which my venerated and now defunct grandmother used to boil cabbage. Hence the tender associations with which they are fraught. I look upon them, day and night, with never-tiring admiration (F). The rings of Saturn and the splendors of Mars are really as nothing to these irridescent vehicles of science. I have, indeed, commenced a poem about them—in humble imitation of the great engineer's favorite bard. It will be comprised in four hundred cantos, commencing thus:

The D——n dash-pots are gleaming like gold,
And are brimming with oil as full as they 'll hold;
Neither odor nor sheen more delightful could be—
They are pungent to smell and refulgent to see.
Diddle dol de! diddle dol de!
O the D——n dash-pot's the dash-pot for me.

"There is, however, another feature in this engine, which illustrates to still greater advantage the grandeur of D——n's inventive genius. That is, the LINK-MOTION. The lustre of this device outshines even

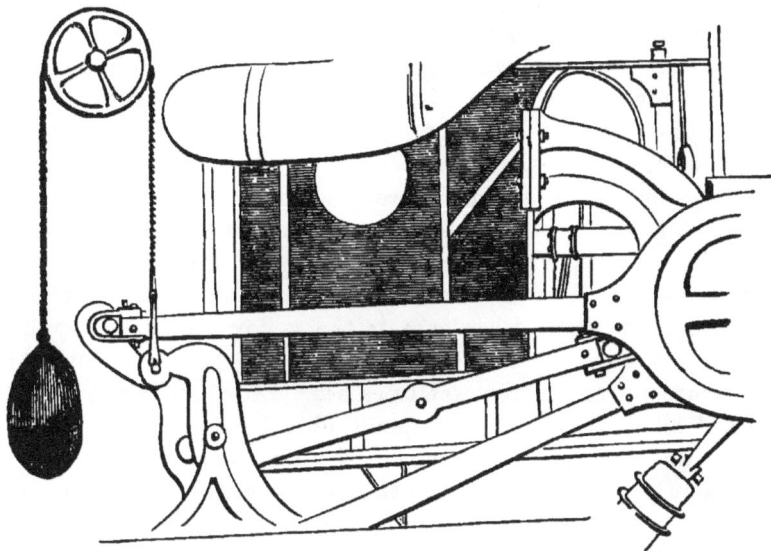

The Grand Link-Motion.

the lustre of the dash-pots. You have just seen something of its achievements in starting this ship. It is not, like the common and vulgar link-motion in general use, an instantaneously adjustible apparatus, easily worked by one man. On the contrary, it requires only about fifteen men to work it, and it keeps them occupied from ten to twenty minutes in adjusting the various cogs, and cranks, and levers, in conjunction with the cut-off machinery, for going ahead or backing. Plainly enough, science marks this link-motion for its own. Only a man who, like D——n, had read 'Richard the Third,' and 'drank of the pure fountain at its source,' could have devised it. So ponderous is the mass of metal employed, that it necessitates a huge weight, acting—on a principle of sweet simplicity—over a pulley, and attached to the upper part of the arcs of both engines, thereby to lessen what otherwise would be a terrible strain on the ship. I am sure you will sympathize with my admiration for this triumph of skill. There is a great gain, too, in noise by this means—noise so salutary in its impression on the common mind. A free space is made for these weights to run up and down inside the coal bunkers; and so, at the slightest motion of the ship, they create a most exhilarating clatter, harmonizing with the delicious din of the entire engine.

"These little touches evince the philosopher. Common minds would have been content with celerity, safety, and economy, without reference to the ornamental intricacies of science. Not so the expansive D———n. His progress in the realms of thought bears no distant analogy to the wise man's progress in the realms of experience. Youth imagines that the world was made for man. Maturity discovers that man was made for the world. So in mechanism. To the budding and innocent D———n of long ago, it seemed, no doubt, that dash-pots were made for engines. To the full-blown D———n of to-day, it is manifestly clear that engines were made for dash-pots. Hence the noble machinery, with its patent cut-off and astonishing link-motion, that we have here the privilege to observe. It has been constructed under the white light of science, and without the slightest regard to expense. Its dash-pots gleam, in the yellow radiance of polished brass, and its monkey-tails are marshalled like the Assyrian cohorts of the pious Byron. Great facilities are afforded for the soothing influence of oil, and for the consequent liberal dissemination of postal currency and green-backed notes. The whistle is a dear one; but Uncle Samuel (like the old trump that he has always been) pays for it without a murmur, and wins the unqualified approbation of D———n. Could more be wished? I leave it to your judgment as a citizen.

Oil is active.

"You have observed—doubtless with profound amazement—the striking ceremonies with which it is necessary to approach this engine,

on the respective subjects of starting and stopping. This, in itself, is evidence of almost human strength of character. In all experience it has been found that large bodies move slowly—an ancient adage, beautifully illustrated in the case of the *Clara Clarita*. (G.)

Persuading the Link to run up.

" It was D———n who selected the boiler and adapted the machinery of that 'thing of beauty,' at a cost, to the gifted Jerome, of over Twenty-One Thousand Dollars. And she sailed precisely one mile and a quarter in two hours and a half, being ultimately thwarted by a stubborn and unaccommodating tide, at Corlear's Hook. Equally valid is the venerable adage as applied to all D———n engines, with their inevitable *Allen* cut-off. They start slowly; they run with dignity; they stop with due deliberation. In watching this one, I am often reminded of an old gentleman, whose girls I used to flirt with, when I was a boy. A solid old gentleman he was—with the gout, and a purple nose, and staunch conservative views; and he sat by night in his drawing-room, in a marvellous arm-chair, his noble form arrayed in indescribable complications of raiment. 'Good evening, sir,' I used to say to him, on entering the room : 'it's a very cold evening.' And then I turned my attention to the girls. But the old gentleman's brain was an active one; and, after precisely fifteen minutes of preparation, his voice, emerging from many bandages, would be heard to answer, 'Yes, you're right—the evening is very cold.' There was a solidity about that old gentleman, very impressive to me in those days; and there is a similar and equally impressive solidity about this D——n engine. If it has a fault; that fault consists in its insufficient illustration of its erudite author's idea upon the subject of bricks. With that idea he electrified a Washington Jury, in the Mattingly Case, and that idea once fully realized in practice, would electrify the entire mechanical world. Imagine a platform supporting a ton of bricks (H), placed upon the end of a one-inch piston! Transport that image to yonder engine-room, and mark the consequence.

> 'How reason reels !
> O what a miracle to man is man,'

especially when he happens to be such a man as D————n.

Rock-Shaft—Rocking in the Bilge-water.

Here *conticuere omnes,* and the black bottle was circulated. But my eloquent friend, absorbed in the grand theme, soon continued his eulogium.

"The genius of D———n has been otherwise made manifest in four enormous rock-shafts, garnished with numerous parabolic cams, and designed for working the steam-exhaust and cut-off valves. It appears, too, in the valves themselves, upon which all manner of intricate instruments have been ingeniously brought to bear, in order to prevent any abrupt and decisive action that should by chance resemble that of vulgar machinery. I think it was the sublime purpose of D———n, in reference to this engine, that it should display 'neither variableness nor the shadow of turning.' His liberal ingenuity has combined the heavy metals as never heavy metals were combined before. Not only has he contrived a dash-pot, to prevent the slamming of the cut-off valve; but he has devised a lip to cushion on the steam as it is jammed against the valve-seat. I dwell upon these details with a fascinated interest. This valve is plug-shaped. On its outside rim is a ring of metal laid upon the seat, and designed to give lead to this plug-arrangement, by expanding or contracting its circle. You can have no conception of the felicity with which it works, unless you have both seen and heard it. The principle is that of the organ-pedal, while the music—but what words can do justice to the incessant *click, click-up, sh, clickety-click, click-up,* so clear, so distinctly intoned, so soothing to the nervous system! What says the poet Milton?

'Can any mortal mixture of earth's sound,
  Breathe such divine, enchanting ravishment!'

"I think not.

"You will marvel, perhaps, that such surpassing excellence of mechanism is not more widely appreciated in this scientific generation. I must remind you of Galileo who was incarcerated for his intelligence; and of the Scottish inventor of umbrellas, who was pelted in the streets for bearing up one of his own anti-pluvial protectors. It was not easy for even the mighty D———n to persuade Uncle Samuel to buy the whistle. The very machinery itself—coy and modest under the eye of distrustful observation—declined at first to operate. I recall the trial day of the Pensa.

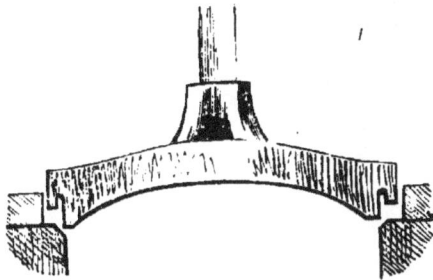

Cut off Valve.

cola. The great engineer himself was on board, to superintend the engine. All was excitement. Promptly, at the word of command, the

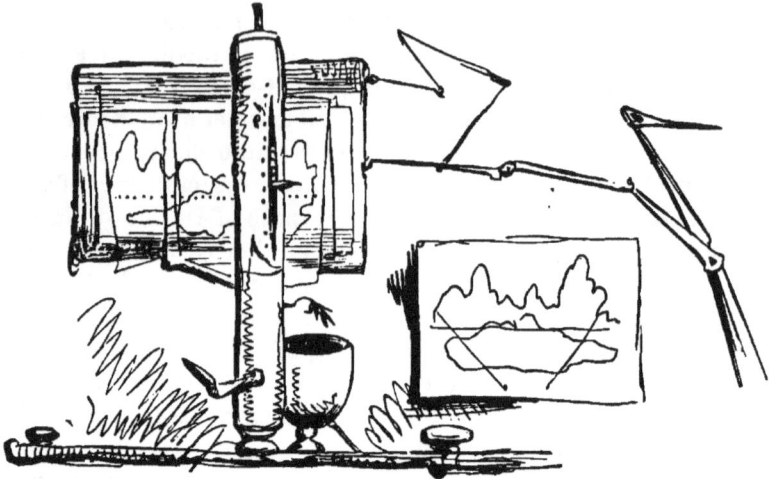

Perfectly clear Indicator and Diagram.—A triumph of genius.

dash-pot phalanx seized their implements, and rushed into action. Gallant charge ! I beheld it from my station at the valves, and thought that I had never seen a more extraordinary proceeding towards an engine. We made, I think, some ninety odd trials before the link would

Gallant charge of the Dash-pot Light Guard.

rise, and the desired, and I may say, indispensable vacuum, consent to form. Coyness, as I have said, is the vice of this wonderful engine;

Working Water-valves—A recreation in hot weather.

but, to cull once more from those sweet pastures of song in which its inventor loves to ramble,

'E'en its vices lean to virtue's side.'

I have since noticed other manifestations of that coyness. For example, this ship has excellent lines for sailing. With a ten-knot breeze, she can out-sail her modest engines entirely. They are sensitive and sluggish under ordinary treatment. We have sometimes made nine knots an hour, with the vessel under sail, and the engines doing their utmost. That was brilliant! But coyness would seem to settle upon those cogs, and paralyze those dash-pots; and then we have disconnected the propeller, and so made eleven-and-a-half or twelve knots under the same amount of sail. At such times, the engine may have attained from forty to forty-four revolutions, cutting off, as indicated by the cut-off dial, at three and one-tenth of the stroke. Steam, as you know, soon works off; but by using the best of coal, and keeping the firemen in a state of incessant and wholesome activity, we have managed to keep up fourteen pounds; which implies that, under certain circumstances, a great number of revolutions may be attained by dragging the propeller through the water as you bowl merrily along.

E

T. M———n (loq.)—She wont work, sir. Can't get her to go over 30, no how.

D———n.—Well—er—give her oil, and shut off three more furnaces,—and—a—oil the wiper—and—slack off a blade of the propeller,—and—scour those dash-pots—and shut the throttle—and—yes, set the clock back.

Engineers ordered to report for duty on board the Pensacola.

Cruise finished—They return home.

"And now," said my friend, as we rose from the gun-carriage, " I think your curiosity is sufficiently gratified in reference to the D———n engine with the ——— cut-off. You have seen that it is a tremendous and unparalleled affair, and you cannot doubt that its inventor is a tremendous and unparalleled man. How, then, can you censure me for my devotion to science? In such a cause, who would not gladly peril life and limb? I have lost three fingers, as you see, and one eye; and Jenkins has lost an arm. Nor have our compatriots in the great work escaped similar honors of martyrdom. Thus the cause of dash-pots is prospered; and thus, at a continued and most noble sacrifice of oil, time, and human life, Uncle Samuel enjoys and pays for the delicious D———n Whistle. And now, as remarked by Hamlet, when about to assault his respectable uncle, 'Let us go in together!'"

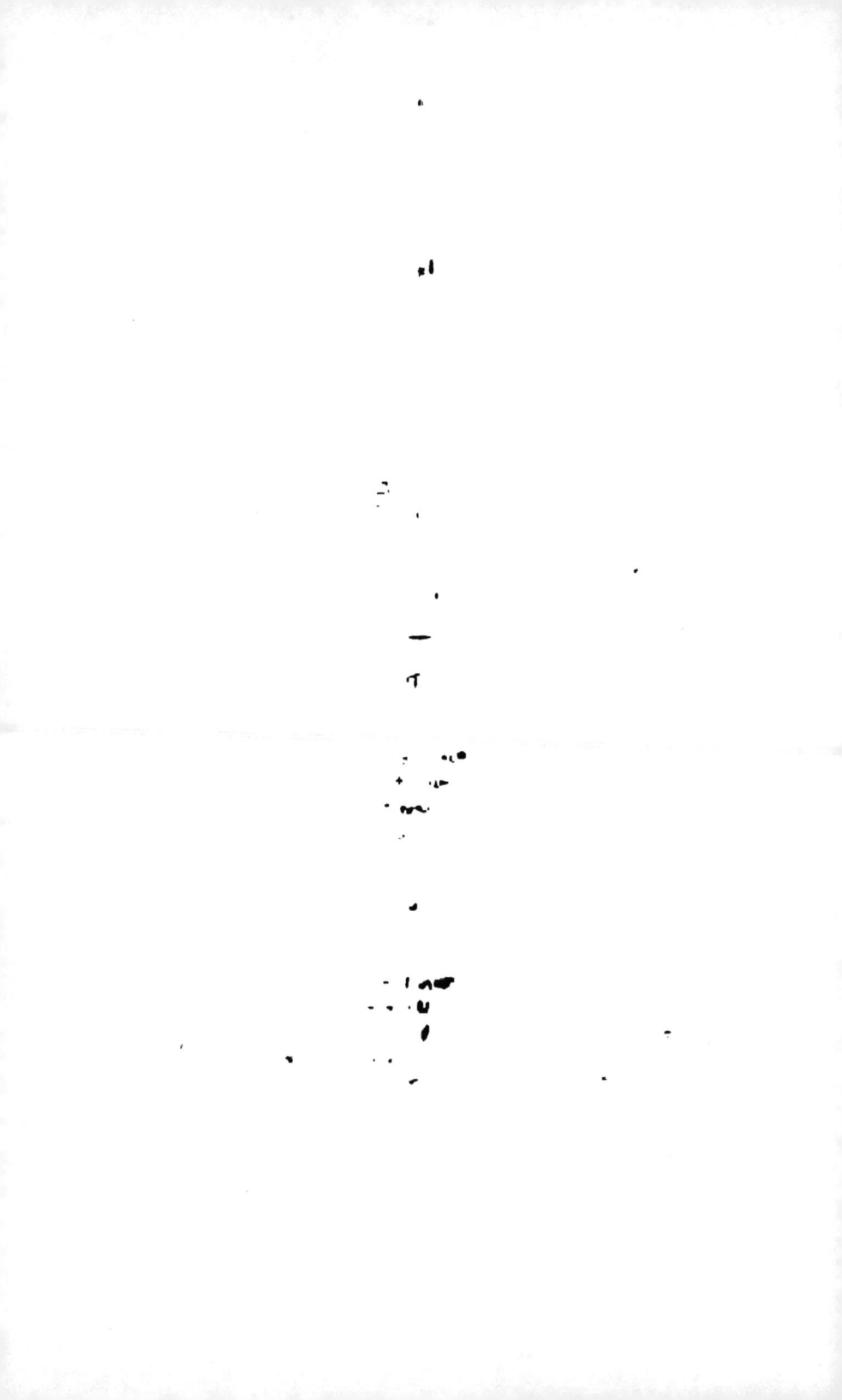

APPENDIX.

(A.)

ISHERWOOD DEFINED.—Ignorance and corruption—Nonsense—Snug, the Joiner—Audacity and impudence—False and not ignorant—Entirely ignorant—Utterly worthless ignoramus—The bull who took a fancy to stop a locomotive—Intriguer—Juggler—Fool—Swindler—Penny-a-liner—Bare-faced fraud—Monumental brass—Villain—Source of utter demoralization—Iago and Uriah Heep—Rascality—The son of a poor widow.—*Speech of — — D——n in the Mattingly Case*, pp. 3, 5, 12, 25, 30, 31, 32, 34, 43, 49, 60, 70, 73, 77, 79.

(B.)

"The contract was awarded to Messrs. D——n and ——. . . . . By the terms of the contract the engine was to be fully completed by the 1st day of July, 1857, but the time was subsequently extended until July 1st, 1858, and again until March 1st, 1859, in both cases by and with the consent of the sureties.

"In his report of January 1st, 1858, the engineer of the Board reported, 'that a considerable portion of the parts of the new engine have been received, and the contractors expect soon to commence the erection of the engine. The new engine house is enclosed, and every thing is prepared for the erection of the engine, and that he saw no reason to doubt that every thing on the part of the contractors would be fully carried out during the life of the contract.' But, on the 1st of January, 1859, we had to report to you that the engine had not been completed, and the engineer reported to us that the work on the new engine was not as far advanced as it was anticipated it would be. The cylinders had been set. No further portions of the work had been received during the season, but a large amount of work in New York was out and nearly ready for shipment. The contractors had notified him that they had made arrangements to send the work forward by rail at once. Still, the 1st of January, 1860, came, and we were again compelled to report to you the engine uncompleted; but our engineer reported to us that the erection of the engine was nearly completed, and the boilers were placed and ready for the setting.

"During all this protracted and vexatious delay in getting this engine into service, which was deemed essential to the safety of the city, and to ensure an uninterrupted supply of water, the confidence of the engineer remained unshaken in its success, and until last summer the Board had repeated assurances from the contractors and their agent, that it would be completed and brought into use in a very short time.

"On the 1st of January, 1861, we were compelled to report to you that the engine had not yet been offered us for acceptance, although the engineer in charge of setting it up represented it as nearly completed, and that he was then at the East, with the avowed purpose of consulting his employers, the contractors, in regard to getting it into operation. On his return, in the month of February, he resumed work on it, and, after making some changes in parts of it, steam was got up, and the engine made short runs occasionally until the 14th of May. When it became necessary to throw engine No. 2 out of use, for the purpose of making important improvements on it, the engineer consented to keep up a supply of water with the new engine during the time our engine was being prepared. Engine No. 2 was out of use a longer time than it was expected it would be, and was not again brought into service until the 1st day of June last.

" Subsequently the new engine was thoroughly overhauled, rollers were removed, and slides substituted, and, after making several short runs, the engineer in charge closed the house, and left for the city of New York, taking with him the keys of the engine house, to report to his employers. Shortly after this, in the month of August last, the keys of the house were returned to the Secretary of the Board, by express, and the President of the Board received a communication from Mr. —— D———n, one of the contractors, apprizing him that the keys had been returned as above, and with an intimation that the contractors would probably abandon their intention of making any further efforts to complete the engine."

The above elegant extract was what the seedy inventor read from the "*Tenth Annual Report of the Board of Water Commissioners to the Common Council of the City of Detroit.*"

(C.)

It will be observed that here, as in several other instances, D———n's rage (heroic and noble passion !) against Isherwood breaks out blindly, and causes him to confuse history. It was not until the D———n egg was very nearly hatched, that the offending Isherwood became Chief Engineer. D———n's first conquest— that of Mr. Secretary Toucey—was made with comparative ease. His martyrdom, so touchingly depicted by himself, did not really commence until after the advent of the new order of things, under Mr. Welles.

(D.)

The poem which the great engineer has thus artfully paraphrased is the following peculiarly melodious and fanciful description which commences Lord Byron's " Hebrew Melodies."

She walks in beauty, like the night,
　Of cloudless climes and starry skies;
And all that's best of dark and bright
　Meet in her aspect and her eyes,
Thus mellowed to that tender light,
　Which heaven to gaudy day denies.

One shade the more, one ray the less,
　Had half impaired the nameless grace
Which waves in every raven tress,
　Or softly lightens o'er her face;
Where thoughts serenely sweet express,
　How pure, how dear their dwelling place.

And on that cheek and o'er that brow,
　So soft, so calm, yet eloquent,
The smiles that win, the tints that glow,
　But tell of days in goodness spent;
A mind at peace with all below,
　A heart whose love is innocent.

(E.)

" At this point James Watt, the Shakspeare of mechanics, appeared—a man whose equal as an engineer has not stood on this earth since, nor do I see any prospect that another will come—a man on whose intellect the Almighty had impressed that intuitive knowledge of his great physical truths, as he had impressed upon the intellect of Shakspeare an intuitive knowledge of his great moral truths. He was an humble man in station, but illumined by the light of genius he rose into grandeur which will never fade. . . . . It was James Watt who fought the battles of civil liberty in the earlier part of this century. It was James Watt—not Lord Wellington—who conquered Napoleon. He it was who, by creating that physical power, enabled England to produce out of its internal resources those means by which she sustained herself against the gigantic strength of the great Emperor, and carried on a war that resulted in his overthrow. Had James Watt never lived, the French Emperor would have wiped out from its place in the history of the world, and out of the catalogue of nations, that power and people who now domineer over land and sea. James Watt was the great pillar on which they stood, and he it was who fought the great battles that maintained them in their present position."—*Speech of — — D———n in the Mattingly Case,* pp. 13, 14.

F

(F.)

" I had read the testimony of Isherwood, and appreciated its effect; and when I entered this room, there stood upon that stand one of the cubs of this lion—an engine driver from the Navy Yard—sent here to devour whatever fragments had been left from the destructive meal of the day before. He was a gorgeous creature as he stood before me ; resplendent with gold lace, his delicate white hands unsullied by vile grease, and unhardened by vulgar toil; his magnificent apparel shedding an effulgeance of glory around him, in which the rings of Saturn encircling his arms vied with the splendors of Mars all over his body for supremacy. There he stood as—

> ' The Assyrian came down like the wolf on the fold,
> And his cohorts were gleaming in purple and gold ;
> And the sheen of their spears was like stars on the sea,
> When the blue wave rolls nightly on deep Galilee.'

" I never behold one of these magnificent visions without thinking how striking is the resemblance between an engine driver of the United States Navy of this day and the lilies of the valley. Not, perhaps, from any peculiar modesty which they have in common, but because like them ' they toil not, neither do they spin ; but I say unto you, that Solomon in all his glory was not arrayed like one of these.' "
—*Speech of* — — *D*———*n in the Mattingly Case*, p. 11.

(G.)

Mr. D———n and the Steam Yacht Clara Clarita.

To the Editor of the ————

Mr. D———n publishes in the *Times* of Tuesday last, a statement signed by Mr. Rowland, concerning the responsibility for the machinery of my steam yacht, the *Clara Clarita*, which is so erroneous and unjust that I am compelled to ask you to publish the facts of the case, so far as I know them.

That some one has very grossly blundered in the construction of that machinery, is a fact very well known. In the ship-yards along the East River it is pretty well understood who the blundering party is, but the public are not quite so well advised. Mr. D———n, by the statement alluded to, attempts to fasten the blame upon " *a gentleman* " whom he does not name, but whom he leaves every one reading the article to infer, to be me. Why, after all the trouble and expense he has put me to, he should add this extra charge, I do not know, unless it be that I am done with him, and Mr. Forbes (whom he must mean, if he means any body,) is not. Mr. D———n knows perfectly well that I never had any thing whatever to do with the construction of that machinery. I never gave an order or made a solitary suggestion respecting it. I have simply paid for the work done under his directions. Knowing nothing whatever about steam myself, I entrusted that department of my vessel entirely to the friendly supervision of Mr. Forbes. I did it chiefly to avail myself of the wonderful skill of Mr. Forbes' engineer, Mr. D———n, of whose capabilities in the way of steam I had heard glowing accounts—partly from himself and partly from other people.

Mr. Forbes knew all about my purpose of building a steam yacht from the very beginning, and took a warm and friendly interest in its construction. He knew that I wished it to be reasonably fast, and to be ready for use as soon as possible. He informed me one day that he had found an engine and boiler which might possibly answer our purpose, and that he " would have D———n examine it." A few days after this he informed me that D———n had examined it, and said it *was just what he wanted; that he could adapt it to my yacht, giving her all the power she required.* The engine was thereupon purchased for the sum of $5000, and Mr. D———n proceeded to "adapt" it. The cost of this adaptation, as may be seen by the vouchers from the Continental Iron Works, now in my possession, every dollar of which was expended under the direction of Mr. D———n, is $16,178·03. It can hardly be supposed by any man of sense, that either Mr. Forbes or myself would have purchased this engine had it not been represented as available. Nor could Mr. D———n, as an engineer, have taken in hand the job of *adapting* it, involving such an enormous cost, unless he had thought so likewise.

At last a trial trip was had. I was on board. Mr. D———n worked the engine himself, assisted by Mr. Rowland and Mr. Rowland's fireman. We started from the Continental Works down the river. The day was fine, everything was in order, the model of the boat was pronounced perfection, and we started off with flying colors.

Her machinery alone remained to be tried. To the best of my recollection *we made one mile and a quarter in just two hours and a half.* It was (in point of space) a brief if not a pleasant trip to all on board—including myself—especially considering that I had waited eight months for the adaptation of this machinery. I could have had fifty engines built during this time notwithstanding the "government pressure." We should have proceeded further down the river, but at Corlear's Hook we were driven back—by the tide. *fact*

For several weeks subsequent to that day the vessel was held subject to Mr. D———n's orders for the purpose of making a further trial, and he was repeatedly invited to do so, but would not. He having abandoned her, I called in the aid of two of the best engineers in New York, (next best of course to Mr. D———n,) and a second trial was had, with no better results. The entire machinery of Mr. D———n was condemned as utterly worthless, and is now being sold for old iron.

Some further apology for this note—if further apology is needed—may be found in the statement made by Mr. D———n yesterday in the presence of a number of gentlemen, that *he was not on board when the trial trip was made;* that "it was made by a chap by the name of Vanderbilt, who was a fool." This "chap, Vanderbilt," is the superintending engineer of the Pacific Mail Steamship Company.

Yours, &c.,

LEONARD W. JEROME.

To the Editor of the Times:

. As Mr. D———n has seen fit, in your paper of this date, to refer to a conversation had with me at the Union Club, on the subject of the machinery of Mr. Jerome's yacht, the *Clara Clarita*, and as his reference to only a portion of the conversation must have arisen from a supposition that the remainder was immaterial to the question, I deem it but proper, both in justice to truth as well as to Mr. D———n's reputation as an engineer, to recapitulate the entire conversation.

Mr. D———n, after stating that the machinery was not such as was calculated to develop satisfactorily the fine qualities of the yacht—but that he was blameless for it, further than regarded its adaptation—answered my inquiry as to what speed could be got out of the vessel with her "adapted machinery" by the reply that she would make 11 to 12 knots an hour, (a statement, by-the-by, which, when I made it to Mr. Jerome, so surprised him as to occasion the exclamation, that "if she could not go faster than that, he would scuttle her.) But, continued Mr. D———n, with such machinery as could be put in the boat, giving me the entire control of its construction, I will guarantee a speed of 16 to 17 knots ; and further, the new machinery will require but twenty feet of the length of the vessel, in lieu of the two-thirds of her capacity occupied by the present "adaptation." Now, leaving aside the fact of Mr. D———n's denial that he was present at the trial trip, and that the engine was worked by him, and therefore that its capacities were never fairly tested—the value of which denial may be ascertained by reference to the subjoined correspondence—it appears to me but fair to calculate, that as Mr. Jerome's yacht, with an estimated speed of twelve knots, went at the extraordinary rate of about half a knot, until she met the tide, when she went backward, it appears, I say, but fair to calculate that with Mr. D———n's improved machinery, she would not have gone much faster than Mr. D———n's minimum of steam success, a government vessel. In conclusion, I fear that when Mr. D———n admitted, for the purpose of his discussion with the Navy Department, that he was "profoundly ignorant of a steam engine, and supposed a cylinder-head to be a full moon," he made an admission of which it will be extremely difficult to disabuse the public, if his future engineering efforts continue to be crowned with the brilliant success of his "adaptation" of the machinery of the *Clara Clarita*.

Yours, very truly,

E. Riggs.

—

MR. RIGGS TO CAPTAIN SMITH.

NEW YORK, Feb. 8, 1864.

Captain Alex. Smith:

DEAR SIR :—Will you please to state who were on board at the trial trip of the *Clara Clarita*, who worked the engine, who assisted, and about how long you were out?

Yours, &c.,

E. Riggs.

Feb. 8, 1864.

E. Riggs, Esq:

DEAR SIR :—In reply to your favor of this date, I would state that there was on board the *Clara Clarita* on her trial trip, Mr. D———n, Mr. T. F. Rowland, and Warren E. Hill, of the Continental Works; Mr. Foulkes, the builder of the yacht; Mr. Jerome, the owner; Mr. Wm. Rowland, the joiner; some of the mechanics of the Continental Works, and the ship's company for the day.

We were underway two hours and a half, the engine being run by Mr. D———n, assisted by Messrs. Hill and Rowland.

This, I believe, answers all your questions, yet I beg to add, that which seemed to me important, viz : that five weeks previously, I was instructed to get up steam, which I did, and Mr. D———n worked the engine at the dock several hours.

I also desire to inform you that on Saturday last, in a conversation with Mr. T. F. Rowland, of the Continental Works, he informed me that what Mr. Jerome had written (referring to his communication in the *Times* of Saturday last) was all true. I have been in command of the *Clara Clarita* since the 18th day of August last, and I have never known any thing to have been done appertaining to her machinery, except under the direction of Mr. D———n. For so small a matter as a bilge-pump, which I required, Mr. Rowland informed me that he would be obliged to consult Mr. D———n.

Yours, &c.,

ALEX. M. SMITH,
Commanding Yacht Clara Clarita.

(H.)

" I will suppose a little cylinder, one inch in diameter, and of indefinite length, and a piston fitting in it, steam-tight, but without friction ; and I will further suppose a cubic inch of water to be passed into the bottom of that cylinder, and the piston to be then let down on the water ; and I will suppose that on the top of that piston there is a platform carrying a ton weight of bricks. "—*D———n's speech in the Mattingly Case,* p. 16.

www.ingramcontent.com/pod-product-compliance
Lightning Source LLC
Chambersburg PA
CBHW032140080426
42733CB00008B/1138